To my heart, my angel, the woman who has fought for me from the very beginning, love conceptualized.

And to one of my closest friends, Juan, thank you for loving me at a time when I found it difficult to love myself and always being honest with me about my writing.

Dark Love

I Want You to Spend the Night

At Times Like These

Three Letters to a Black Man

Conversations Like These

Kamaria

Lie

Mornings, Coffee, and Strings

Love Me

She

Nat Turner

When Love…

Unrequited

Waiting

Bad Bitch Barbie

Confessions of a Weekend Alcoholic

Cotton

Loving Him

Intro

These are not love poems. These poems are not focused on one person or fixated on heartbreak, but rather an observation of love. Honest input from a writer who openly admits her struggle with the concept.

"She had been in her room all day. She meticulously erased the bubble gum pink wallpaper with the dancing teddy bear trim. She reimagined a tiny house. Everything she needed within the walls of her bedroom. A small cooler in the corner supplied with apple juice boxes. A pantry right beside it stocked with Graham crackers. She had her bed, a boom box and about 15 CDs, it even played the radio. There was a TV directly in front of her bed. Her bed. It was the most pivotal part of her plan. This is where she felt safest. This is where she'd taken it upon herself to lay between pastel colored sheets until her release. As long as all of her limbs remained on the mattress and underneath her bed set she was safe. If so much as a wisp of air raised a hair on her skin she was exposed. She planned on being wrapped in safeness until her mother came home.
"Hey come here!" The voice for which the plan was created. The reason why she was in hiding. Ever so quiet, as to not disturb him.
But she left safe. She left carpet for hard wood floors like unfamiliarity under her bare feet. Coke like cans read 'Corona' piled at the base of the couch.
"Yes...sir" every part of her just wanting to be wrapped in her linen cocoon again.
"Your mother's crazy...you know that right? She threw that telephone at my head. You know I could have her arrested for that? Do you know where she went?"
"No..."
"Of course you don't. You're always going to take her side. You look just like her too....I hope you don't share her temper....fucking crazy...."

Tears burst through her body in the form of anger. She wanted her mother to come back and go to her safe place with her. They would never have to leave. She had everything they could ever want there. They would lay in bed and her mother would read stories to her, and they would survive off of Graham crackers and apple juice. He would never touch her again. He could never accidentally push her into walls or lock her out, because nothing bad happened beyond pink wallpaper with dancing bears on the trim.

These are not love poems.

[Un]Conditional

Isake Samiyah Perkinson

Dark Love

Like midnight
Not downtown Atlanta, at the corner of Peters St. and Spring St. SW, on Friday
night midnight
More like 1850, the plains of Oklahoma midnight
Like peaceful and serene midnight
Like a familiar carbon sky that shelters your entire being midnight
Like I've been here before midnight

Like chocolate
The good kind
The one that they sold at the end of the line during Christmas time in the
woman's department of Macy's
The one your mom ate right in front of your face while you nibbled on a candy
cane
The one you save for those nights where the weight of the world has undressed
you within the walls of your apartment
And confined you to a seething hot bubble bath with red wine
The chocolate that's way too delectable to be eaten like candy
Slightly tart with a hint of sweetness

Like beauty
Like going against everything they ever said black love should be
Seeing more beauty in the droplets of sweat raised from African like skin than
this world will ever see
Like brown on brown making a movie
Like I run my fingers through the coils and kinks on your crown
The same coils and kinks mastah would look at and frown
Like you're a king and I'm a queen
Like Dark
Like Love
Like We

I Want You to Spend the Night

I want you to spend the night
I need to know that you'll still be here when I wake
Leave your boxers on the floor
And your shirt at the foot of my bed
I need you to assure me that my beauty has not been orgasmed out of you
That I did not allow you to kiss my insecurities in vain
I am not glass
You will not see my abnormally rapid heartbeat when you touch me
You will not see my lungs nearly collapse while I forget to gasp for air
You will not be able to identify the adrenaline pumping through my veins
But this does not mean that I can't break
And shatter into a million pieces
I can be very fragile at times
So I will wrap myself in uncertainties
And brace myself for the fall
Hold me close
Until dusk and Dawn shake hands like the oldest friends that they are
And sparrows give crickets a chance to rest their eyes
And dew graces each blade of grass

Love me
Like you know why my heart is bandaged
Stitched deep
And fragile
Why 2am sends chills down my spine
And intimacy is wanted, not required

Dear Black Man

1
Dear black men
I love you like you were my own brother
My father
My uncle
You are beautiful to me
Followed in jewelry stores like your melanin is the fee
Have you scrape off that tar it must be a disease
You out in these streets trying to be a man but that shit ain't free
Blue and black around every corner with nigga fever
Catch a nigga like "oops I couldn't see him he was too close the color of the streets"
"It was too dark for me to see"
"My finger tripped over the trigger"
"His midnight made me nervous"
"But shit, he was just another nigger"
These bullets ain't free

2
Dear black man
I'm sorry we've tried to dilute you
Light skin
Hazel eyes
That curly "good" hair
Mama was just afraid my son's would look just like you
Harsh but true
Look at what this world has done to you
Look at all the mamas crying for beautiful black men like you
This world only values your jump shot
And how nice your bars are
Set you on a stage
Sold to the highest bidder
They can watch you better when you're under the spotlight
Feed you off of the limelight
Gold chains are such hard habits to break
They will Kanyeezy you out of the only dream they ever allowed you to have
You're trying to get signed
Too bad they never disclosed that your soul was right above the dotted line
Don't ever give a black man too much ambition

3
Dear black man
I fell in love with you
Slowly and peacefully
Like small suburban bridges running over steady moving streams

Like flowers and love poems
I fell in love with your pain
Your distrust
Your heartache
Your unease
Skin flawless like looking up at the midnight's sky
I fell in love with you because this world never had the intention to
I fell in love with you because you the same brown boys I used to play with on
Malone Street between 4 and 6 pm
Until Mama called us in to eat
And you the same brown boy that fell in love with Pam and created me
And if you don't know Pam then you don't really know me
And you the same brown boy that gave me my first kiss
And told me you loved me
And in the same sense broke my heart...
But I had to understand...
As black women we have to understand
That every brown boy grows up to be a Black Man...

Conversations Like These

Her back has been turned towards me this whole conversation
What else is there to say?
Change of subject
But my thoughts are still processing
I just want to say I'm sorry for not being everything I promised you I'd be
At some point I checked out mentally
So there was nothing you could say at that point to get through to me
Truthfully, I meant every one of those 8 letters I told you last Tuesday
But "I" always comes before "u" in these sentences
Don't turn your back towards me
Shutting me out of everything
It was a lot more complicated than me and you
If it was us I'd ride until the wheels fell off and exposed burnt out rusted rotors
Rust only Sunday morning dew and a crisp latter august air can create
And if it was us I'd give up my Atlanta independence
Follow you half way around the world
Repping flags that you fight for but I struggle to believe in
And if it was us I'd drive my Pontiac 20 hours to your front door to hold you
like warmth and pressure can kill pain
But life hits you so hard sometimes you are forced into adaptation
Granite in metamorphosis
I know why your back was turned away from me
Voice wavering like salt water rhythmically hitting my toe nail beds cradled in
sinking sand
I know why your back is turned, but I'm selfish so I call your name
And your eyes break me

Kamaria

I find it funny how you are blissfully unaware of your profound beauty
Your gentle nature
Your caring heart
Your honesty is like a waterfall fed by the Nile River
Your smile like the moon when it only shows one eighth of its glory
Yet still manages to illuminate the world
You see beauty where they saw tragedy
They said tragic when they couldn't understand your beauty
Like persecuting a caterpillar for creating a cocoon
Like years of pressure doesn't give way to a diamond
You are the rarest of gems
A renaissance beauty
The kind that puts butterflies in my stomach
Questions in my mind
And an eternal smile upon my face

Tell me a lie
Tell me that you fucking love me and you need me
That blue and red don't make purple
And that your heart is the heart that pumps life through my veins
That breaking hearts is somehow vindicating
And your inconsistencies are attractive
Tell me a good lie

Mornings, Coffee, and Strings

I think about you more and more these days
Is it wrong I wish for early hazelnut scented mornings?
You slouched into one of our wooden kitchen chairs
More like pine than mahogany
More like mahogany surrounding the strings of your other leading lady
More like making love to her chords
More like summoning me from upstairs
I allow my feet to embrace the coldness of the granite floors
You play so melodically, so calm
Is it wrong that all I want to do is wrap you in my arms?
My fingers tracing your skin so lightly as to not disturb your beauty
Is it wrong that you're that beautiful to me?

Love Me

Love me.
Until you can't anymore
Until the soil has absorbed all of the blood running through your left atrium
When your veins become the meaning of biodegradable
Blueish green
I held your hand so many times
It became second nature
And your temper rose from your knuckles and wrapped around your wrist
The beat of the Bachata just beneath your skin
This is home for me
So I ask you
To love me
Until your cartilage gives birth to new life

Baby's breath was always my favorite
It is sweet and faint
Without being overbearing
And it is often overlooked
Never appreciated for its divine beauty
The filler
Between calla lilies, white roses, wild daisies and tulips
You should make baby's breath
And then I will know you are with me
So you can hold me
Hold me.
Between the branches and the leaves that were carved from your sweat
Even when you are holding me like this you would have still found a way to be midnight
Bark that is more like mahogany
Please be mahogany for me
When waters get high and testy you will have become my anchor
Your branches will never give way
So I will stay and listen

Call me.
In the middle of the night
Through wolves
Mimicking your laugh
I would still recognize it anywhere
It is pure joy wrestling tonsils for airtime
The unexpected in a moment grieved with solemn
Promise me no goodbyes my love

She the type to deal with her demons on her own
2 am crying all alone
About the same people that done her wrong

Nat Turner

Nat always been crazy
Crazy a' hell
So I not be surprised
How things work out
He always been crazy
But he always had a big heart
He seen how massah hurt me
How he have me touch him in places I knows God don't approve
First time he hurt me I bleed right good
I tell mama and she say don't talk about it
But I tell Nat and he wanna go beat massah like a nigger
(Laughter)
Chile! Wouldn't that be somethin?
Ole peach fuzz of a man tellin Nat to stop?!

Yea Nat always been crazy
He told me one night he been talkin to God out in them fields
He say God say it's time to fight
They was callin him a prophet
I call him a dumb ass
Tell him if he fight he gone die like a ignant nigger
That they gon laugh at his grave and let da vultures pick at his bones
But he still kept planning
And I love him so I keep quiet

Nat stole a kiss from me out in the summertime by the water
I's Washin clothes
And he askin me about this and that type foolishness
He say I more beautiful than any of them white girls that live in the house
I know he was lying though
Who would want my nappy braids
When them girls got bouncy curls that come past they shoulders
Skin clear
And they nose sit upright
But I kiss that fool back

Like I say before, Nat always been crazy
So I ain't surprised he went and killed them white people
But Nat always been special too
So I really ain't surprised them niggers followed him

When Love...

When love fucks you over and you find yourself writing poems again
And not giving a fuck again
And all the women in your phone are likeable enough for you to keep going
back to

You even kind of love them after a few shots of jack and henny
....wait no....they always ruin the facade with their all too often eager words

And you can't explain to her that she's not her
Her being the love of your life
But you hate her
And that's why you're sleeping with she right now
But she will want more eventually and you can't explain that you left your heart
in loves hands and forgot to get it back
So when she sheds tears and asks why, you'll just shrug and tell her "it is what
it is"

Because when love fucks you over you'll begin to convince yourself that you
are over it
Over the need for companionship
You will believe it so much, it will become true most days
You won't think of her
And you'll sleep with she
And you'll focus on you
The repetitive call for love will be muffled like water that's been dripping for a
month straight

Your poems will become empowering
As if you're trying to prove to your readers that at one point that person didn't
mean the world to you

Unrequited

For all the men who never received the reciprocity of an 'I love you'...
She a soot ridden diamond
Who has not had the time nor pressure to mature yet
You bought her two hotdogs, a bag of cheddar cheese ruffles, and an orange
Fanta on your first date
I guess it makes sense now
The bitch only consumes those things that are not good for her
She told you she met someone
Like a bff?
Bffe?
Best friend forever and eternity?
That orgasm was never a ring my nigga....
This woman was never a queen my nigga
Save yourself, just get up and leave my nigga

Waiting

Blue
Like padded walls
Like I've lost all credibility
Because of the magazines sitting in front of me
Cold air hitting the back of my neck
Hairs standing on edge
I am shivering uncontrollably
And I pray God has not sent his angels to look at me
But rather to comfort me

Mind numb
Heart racing rapidly
Pools of sweat collecting at the arch in my back
Water?
I need some
Maybe it's not too late to go back

Because I remember being a 3 year old
Whose mom and dad are twenty somethings?
Who hate each other so much they claim its love
And yelling matches are frequent in their house
And your mom tells you to call the police on your dad
But she picks up the phone and throws it at him instead

Because I'm twenty something
And I struggle with happiness everyday

And he's twenty something and has no secure plans

And we love each other just enough to call it hate

And I'm cold
And I might as well be alone
Because nobody knows you're here
I'm sitting in this chair, and its one seat per two heart beats
And every moment I think I can love you
I become more certain that I can't

So I'm sorry that I'm twenty something and have a hard time comprehending
love
And this waiting room is blue....like padded walls

Bad Bitch Barbie

Bad Bitch Barbie
Yes it's back for a limited time only
Only 19.99
Yes the one the only
Bad Bitch Barbie
For only a few dollars extra she will twerk to your favorite trap song
Shot glasses included
Each Barbie comes with their own personal bottle of peach Cîroc
Poles sold separately

Watch Barbie count ones and then take them to the nearest Michael Kors store
"Store sold separately"
Get her a matching wallet and purse
Goes perfectly with Barbie's leggings and cheetah...I mean leopard print bra
Yes this is classy
It's Barbie

Hurry and call now and you'll be able to go home with the special edition 30
inch 100% Malaysian bad bitch Barbie
Watch as she accidentally sits on her extensions
Uh oh Barbie
No worries, cheer Barbie up by filling in her eyebrows
Highlight, highlight, contour
All Barbie's resemble Kim K

And wait! There's more!
Bad Bitch Barbie goes to the plastic surgeon!
We'll throw in removable butt implants that you're sure to have hours of fun
with
When you're finished, strip Barbie down and have a photo shoot with Ken
All Barbie's can be models too

Bad Bitch Barbie comes in a wide variety
Team dark skin
Team light skin
And the most coveted foreign chick to ease any man's anxieties

Hurry and get them while they last
Only 19.99!!
We accept 'Lack of self-respect', 'Low self-esteem', 'Unoriginal thoughts', and
Visa....

Confessions of a weekend alcoholic....

Why the fuck am I doing this shit again
The last time was supposed to be the last time
I am my own inebriated lover this time
Henny rolls down my tongue like entrance is not a crime
Burned a hole in my soul where jack was supposed to lie
I hear conversations yet I can't open my eyes
Because my sober mind won't lie
I heard it all last night
My arm is like the claw crane that never graced you with toys
"Mom can I have another quarter?" -Ass boy
Not being able to wrap myself in my skin properly
My insecurities down the slot machine
Yes, I'm trying to pick up another drink
I like the way I feel
I hate the way it tastes
Just come here so I can whisper more confessions in your ear
She says I'll only tell her I love her after my 4th shot
Why you got to hear it?
You should know I fucking love you a lot
Maybe not
But everyone wants to feel love when they're on a strange tile floor
Around 4
And porcelain never felt this good around Christmas time, draped in American
girls finest
Lay my head against it
I'm cooler than the wine is
Let me laugh uncontrollably about the saddest shit in the world
That way you won't know I'm hurting
Beer will reveal your pain
Like you just got to revisit this shit Saturday through Sunday
Got the room spinning away
And that idiotic smile on your face is all for play
The 48 hour bit
Jonny Carson would probably just quit
You're fucked up and everybody knows it

Cotton

US currency is 75 percent cotton and 25 percent linen fibers
150 years after slavery was abolished she is still on her knees picking cotton for
rich old white men
Just like her greatest grandmother
Irony at its finest

She is serenaded by whiskey scented lullabies in the hours when children are
tucked into bed while their mothers cry themselves to sleep, alone, again
"You're beautiful" eventually loses all motivation when uttered with cotton
pasted to the palms of their hands, like kindergarteners tacking macaroni to a
poster board
It never seems to stay there
Soon "you're beautiful" will morph into 'shake that ass bitch" and cotton will
rain over her naked body
Saartjie Baartman kind of thick
Twerking is provocative when most of your weight is carried in your hips
See if Miley Cyrus would get ostracized like this
Weight of the world type thick

She doesn't mind
Even with her whole body being exposed they still can't see the scars
She picks cotton for a living
Just like her greatest grandmother
Slap that ass....
She's getting whipped for free

Loving Him

She loved him
From across the room
Amongst Crayola markers
Finger paintings
Snotty noise peers
That spoke in such a high pitched tone they could pierce the very workings of
your ears
Amongst smiley faced stickers
That eternally grinned upon letters to parents of the unloved
From concerned teachers who attempted to love the unloved
But it was impossible because, how could the unloved be loved if they never
knew what love was?
Amongst the assortment of story books
Empty Elmer's Glue bottles
And Cheetos prints lining the side of tables
Remnants of that days lunch

She loved him
Even though she wasn't quite sure what love was
Satisfied with an unrequited relationship
She had a "boyfriend"
That she officially said "Hi" and "Bye" to everyday
However, in the depths of her mind they shared the whole world together
He barely knew her name
But she knew his date of birth
October twentieth 1993 to be exact
And his shellfish allergy
His asthma
Number two on his little league football team where he played safety
And she knew that they could be together
Keeping their relationship intact
For twenty years, four months, and five days
When they would meet at the end of the aisle

Exactly fifteen years, nine months, two weeks, and three days later when she no
longer loved him
When she no longer loved him
When she loved another
Not much had changed
Still satisfied with an unrequited relationship
Not truly knowing what love is
When he barely knew her phone number by heart
And she loved him
Amongst the clean white sheets
The generic paintings hung on the stark white walls
Amongst his Nikes left on the floor

His t-shirt laid across the chair
The complimentary bottles of shampoo and conditioner
That were never used
Because he never stayed long enough to take a morning shower
Eat the morning breakfast by way of room service
And she still loved him
And it was ok that he always had to go to work early
Leaving her heart just as empty as the condom packets left on the dresser top
the night before
And her soul just as stale as the hotel room she would be forced to check out of
in exactly one hour, twenty-eight minutes, and two seconds
She loved him
And when he called in two days at 11:59 pm
She would answer and they would do it all over again
And he would whisper in her ear "I love you"
And she would believe him
Because she loved him
And even though he barely knew her phone number by heart
She would rather love him
Than to ever love herself
And be alone